# THE (YOUNG) ANTIRACIST'S WORKBOOK

## Questions for Changemakers

### IBRAM X. KENDI
### +
### NIC STONE

ONE WORLD

New York

# INTRODUCTION

On November 23, 2012, a young man named Jordan Davis was murdered at a gas station over the volume and type of music booming from the SUV he was riding in with some friends. He was 17 years old, unarmed, and African American.

I was living abroad in Jerusalem, Israel, at the time, and I'd recently—five months prior to be exact—given birth to my first child: a little Black boy who was given a name that means "beam of light." And he was light to me. So, to hear of this older Black boy, the precise type of boy *my* boy would likely become, losing his life over something that seemed so trivial? The story crawled down into my blood and pulsed through me with every heartbeat.

I wanted to know: *Why?* Why would this grown man pull out a gun and fire it into a car filled with teenagers? What about them could've been so menacing? Was it their literal Black bodies? The clothes they wore and the style in which they wore them? Had they spoken to him using words he didn't like? Was it the music itself?

I looked at my kid, and then I looked at the world. And it hit me—hard—how much of a disadvantage my sweet baby boy would be at just because he was born in his particular body. And I got angry, yes...but more important, I heard that pivotal question again:

*WHY?* My presumption is that if you're reading this introduction, you plan to utilize this book. Because you've begun to explore not only the *Why?* but also the *How? When?* and *Where?* of racism, and now you're trying to figure out *What?* to do. (And I will say, if you haven't read the book this workbook is based on—*How to Be a (Young) Antiracist* by Dr. Ibram X. Kendi and yours truly, Nic Stone—it wouldn't be a bad idea to go through that first and foremost.)

In which case: I salute you. You have made the conscious decision to embark on what is likely to be an uncomfortable journey. No matter *what* your background is, it takes courage to care. Especially for those who are different from you.

I also want to express my gratitude: This fight against racism isn't easy, and as a person who would greatly benefit from some large-scale changes to various types of policy, I can't thank you enough for your willingness to actively participate even when it comes to the thoughts and ideas you share with others who are not necessarily engaged in antiracist work.

Long story short, if you are engaging with this workbook because you have chosen (or even are *considering*) a life of antiracism, you are a treasure. And I truly believe that, with your hands on deck, we can make a better world.

Hopefully one where boys like mine (there are two of them now) are free and able to play their music loud with abandon.

**—NIC STONE**

"WE EITHER PERPETUATE THROUGH SILENCE—OR OPPOSE IT AT EVERY

—IBRAM X. KENDI AND NIC STONE, *HOW TO BE A (YOUNG) ANTIRACIST*

RACISM—EVEN
WE CHOOSE TO
OPPORTUNITY. "

# LEARN

The book that accompanies this journal, *How to Be a (Young) Antiracist* by Ibram X. Kendi and Nic Stone, embraces learning as a lifelong journey. *How to Be a (Young) Antiracist* is Stone's adaptation of Dr. Kendi's international best-selling book *How to Be an Antiracist*, a paradigm-shifting memoir that explores racism through the author's eyes as a historian and a Black man in today's world. He writes about race, equity, and practical action from a historic and personal perspective, offering readers the chance to learn and make change alongside him.

This workbook is an extension of Dr. Kendi's ongoing endeavor. This is *your* chance to examine the world around you with a critical eye and decide how *you* can make a positive difference in your world. But before we act, we must learn. So, here goes nothin'.

# Before we get into the nitty-gritty . . .

Who are *you*? How do you identify? What experiences do you bring to this book?

Hint: In addition to race, this workbook explores *a lot* of facets of a person's identity. Think about your culture, the ways you express yourself, your age, religion, education—everything!

# Think of a time when you felt really cool, powerful, and comfortable in your own skin, like Ibram at the beginning of *How to Be a (Young) Antiracist.*

What were you wearing? How were you behaving? What particular activities or mannerisms were you performing? Do you think it matched up to the expectations people had of you? Did this matter to you? Why or why not?

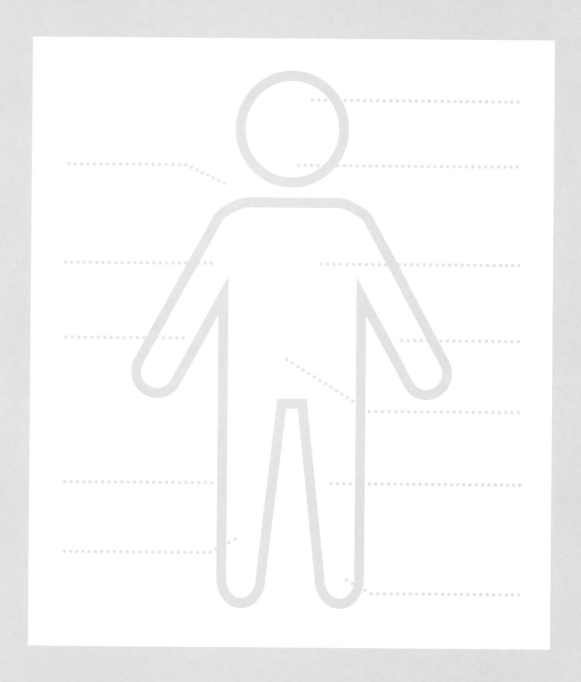

Fill out this illustration with characteristics you love about each part of yourself, whether it be personality traits, strengths you associate with each body part, or activities each body part helps you perform.

**Have you ever entered a space and felt the atmosphere change instantly? Or have you ever joined a group of people and noticed that you were the only one with something different about you? How did you feel?**

_____

_____

_____

_____

_____

_____

_____

_____

_____

_____

"It's important to *see* and *acknowledge* that people look different and are categorized accordingly so you can *see* and *acknowledge* that people are treated differently based on those categories. The goal of antiracism isn't to *erase* color differences, but to detach harmful ideas about races and racial groups from the colors we see. One either believes problems are rooted in groups of people/characteristics of racial groups or sees the roots of problems in power and policies that uphold racial inequity. We can let racism stand, or we can stand against it."

Understanding racism is like examining the strata of a rock formation—the closer you look at the inequities among different racial groups, the more complex it gets. You begin to understand how power influences policy, policy influences ideas, and ideas influence actions. Your worldview might shift as you learn about the history of race and racism . . . and it might feel really hard to wrap your head around what you learn. It might not sit well with you emotionally.

You might need to take breaks while doing this work, and *that's okay*.

**How do you feel now?**

_____

_____

_____

_____

**How do you want to feel at the end of this workbook?**

_____

_____

_____

_____

**What do you hope to get out of this workbook?**

_____

_____

_____

_____

# DEFINITIONS: ANTIRACIST EDITION

Definitions are anchors that give us a place to start—a place to start pursuing change.

Before we go any further, take some time to read the following terms. Think about what each word means to you—what it is, what it is *not*, what it represents in your everyday life—and then, compare your definitions with Dr. Kendi's on page 19.

Check out the glossary of even more definitions on pages 151–55 to learn about other important terms you might come across in your antiracist work.

## RACE

## RACISM

## RACIST (adjective)

**ANTIRACISM**

**ANTIRACIST** (adjective)

**ANTIRACIST** (noun)

**RACIST** is more an adjective than a noun, and it's not an insult; anyone who takes it as an insult or tries to use it as one likely doesn't know what the word actually means.

   (That's right. There's no definition for *racist* as a noun because, while this word is frequently utilized as a noun, for our purposes, it makes more sense as an adjective. So let's just stick to that here.)

**RACE** A socially sustained power construct created to separate and define collections of people based on observable, shared characteristics.

**RACISM** A powerful collection of policies that sustains racial inequities and is substantiated by ideas of racial hierarchy. Also known as *institutional racism, structural racism*, and *systemic racism*.

**RACIST** (adjective): In support of a racist policy through action or inaction, or expressing a racist idea, both of which produce and normalize racial inequities.

**ANTIRACISM** A powerful collection of policies that lead to racial equity and are substantiated by ideas of racial equality.

**ANTIRACIST** (adjective): Supporting an antiracist policy through actions or inaction, or expressing an antiracist idea, both of which produce and normalize racial equity.

**ANTIRACIST** (noun): One who makes the conscious decision to support or enact policies, and expresses ideas that produce and normalize racial equity, while denouncing, pointing out, and standing against policies and ideas that sustain racial inequity and injustice.

As you dig into this workbook and any books, podcasts, movies, or other media that deal with race and antiracism, you may come across terms you don't quite understand. Keep a list of those terms here, and when you have the chance, discuss or research the terms—you might enlist the help of a trusted adult or friend, too.

_____      _____

_____      _____

_____      _____

_____      _____

_____      _____

_____      _____

_____      _____

_____      _____

"DEFINITIONS ANCHOR US IN PURSUABLE PRINCIPLES. THEY GIVE US A JUMPING-OFF POINT FOR DESCRIBING THE WORLD AND OUR PLACE IN IT USING STABLE AND CONSISTENT LANGUAGE SO THAT WE'RE 1. ALL UNDERSTANDING A THING IN THE SAME WAY, AND 2. ABLE TO WORK TOWARD SHARED STABLE AND CONSISTENT GOALS."

The authors of *How to Be a (Young) Antiracist* firmly believe in the power of language—that definitions anchor us in pursuable principles. Use this space to create a web of words, labels, feelings, thoughts, and definitions that anchor *you*. Add more lines and bubbles if you need to.

How do you
define yourself?

Your closest relationships?

Your culture?

Your values?

Your goals?

ME

Definitions, beliefs, and big ideas are often handed down from generation to generation, without being examined, questioned, or reimagined.

This idea is reflected when Dr. Kendi shares the story of his Martin Luther King Jr. speech in high school. Read the passage on the right—an excerpt from Dr. Kendi's speech—and underline or highlight the racist ideas he spoke to his community.

Why do you think he believed these things? Why do you think the Black people present applauded his speech?

_____

_____

_____

_____

What would be Dr. King's message for the millennium?

_____

_____

_____

_____

## LET'S VISUALIZE AN ANGRY 71-YEAR-OLD DR. KING:

"It was joyous, our emancipation from enslavement . . . but . . .

now, 135 years later, the Negro is still not free . . .

Our youths' minds are still in captivity!

They think it's okay to be those who are most feared in our society!

They think it's okay not to think!

They think it's okay to climb the high tree of pregnancy!

They think it's okay to confine their dreams to sports and music!

Their minds are being held captive, and our adults' minds are right

there beside them.

Because they somehow think that the cultural revolution that began on

the day of my dream's birth is over.

How can it be over when many times we are unsuccessful because

we lack intestinal fortitude?

How can it be over when our kids leave their houses not knowing how

to make themselves, only knowing how to not make themselves?

How can it be over if all of this is happening in our community?

So I say to you, my friends, that even though this cultural revolution

may never be over,

## I STILL HAVE A DREAM . . . "

**Is it possible for people of color to be racist? Why or why not?**

"THAT'S THE THING ABOUT RACIST IDEAS: THEY MAKE PEOPLE OF COLOR THINK LESS OF THEMSELVES ... WHICH MAKES THEM MORE VULNERABLE TO RACIST IDEAS.... AND THEN ON THE FLIP SIDE, THE SAME RACIST IDEAS MAKE WHITE PEOPLE THINK *MORE* OF THEMSELVES, WHICH FURTHER ATTRACTS THEM TO RACIST IDEAS. AND ALL OF THIS TENDS TO HAPPEN INSIDE OF PEOPLE WITHOUT ANYONE REALIZING IT."

**Why do some people claim "reverse discrimination" is a thing? (*Is it a thing?*)**

_____

_____

_____

_____

_____

_____

_____

_____

_____

_____

_____

_____

**How are beliefs passed down and internalized?**

_____

_____

_____

_____

_____

_____

**How do we know which stories or beliefs we need to analyze with a critical lens?**

_____

_____

_____

_____

_____

_____

What is the difference between *equity* and *equality*? Read the definitions for **RACIAL EQUITY** and **RACIAL INEQUITY** below. Maybe look up *equity* and *equality* in the dictionary, too. Consider discussing this with a small group of friends or a trusted adult to get their take on these terms.

## RACIAL EQUITY

When two or more racial groups are standing on relatively equal footing and experience similar and/or equal outcomes.

## RACIAL INEQUITY

When two or more racial groups are not standing on relatively equal footing.

## In *How to Be a (Young) Antiracist*, the authors share some statistics reflecting racial inequities the United States:

- In 2014, 71 percent of White families lived in houses they owned, compared to 45 percent of Latinx families and 41 percent of Black families.

- Life expectancy for White people is 3.5 years longer than that of Black people, and the infant mortality rate for Black babies is double that of White babies.

- African Americans are 25 percent more likely to die from cancer than White Americans.

**LIST FIVE OTHER EXAMPLES OF RACIAL INEQUITIES:**

1.

2.

3.

4.

5.

# Is there such a thing as neutrality in the fight against racism? Why or why not?

"EVENTUALLY, BY BECOMING ANTIRACIST— SEEING ALL RACIAL GROUPS AS EQUAL AND CAPABLE OF THRIVING WITHOUT NEEDING TO DEVELOP TO MEET ANY ONE STANDARD—YOU WILL BECOME FREE. THEN YOU'LL HELP FREE OTHERS BY OPENING *THEIR* EYES TO WHAT YOU SEE."

**PRESIDENT LYNDON B. JOHNSON** once said,

"You do not take a person who, for years, has been hobbled by chains and liberate him, bring him up to the starting line of a race, and then say, 'You are free to compete with all the others,' and still justly believe that you have been completely fair."

Johnson uses the
metaphor of running
a race to illustrate
how difficult it is
to overcome racial
inequity. Think of
another metaphor for
racial inequity and
draw it here.

# "Unless EVERYONE is going to be given access to the same resources, holding EVERYONE to the same standard is what's *actually* unfair."

What kinds of resources do people of all races and identities need to achieve equity? We all need food, water, and shelter, right? What else?

_____

_____

_____

_____

_____

_____

_____

_____

_____

_____

_____

_____

_____

## What is **EMPATHY**?

## What does empathy have to do with any of this?

## Why is empathy an important tool for any antiracist's toolbox?

# QUICK HISTORY: A Timeline

You might be wondering how "race" and "racism" managed to manifest in *actual* ideas and actions and policies. Drumroll please . . .

Here is a timeline from *How to Be a (Young) Antiracist* that offers a mostly succinct summary of how race relates to power and how racism became a Thing:

## 1400s

Prince Henry the Navigator of Portugal creates the first transatlantic slave-trading policies by using his great wealth to fund Portuguese voyages to West Africa to capture Black bodies for trading. Slavery itself wasn't some newfangled thing: Christian and Islamic traders had been enslaving literally anyone and everyone for-basically-ever. But the Portuguese shifted the human-buying and human-selling to exclusively African bodies.

## 1450s

Henry's nephew Alonso—then king—asks this dude named Gomes de Zurara to write the story of Henry's African adventures down. This is the first transcribed account of perceived Black inferiority. Anybody without "White" skin is deemed ugly and worthy of enslavement, and the Dark-skinned people encountered in Africa are said to have been lost (from a Christian perspective), living "like beasts, without any custom of reasonable beings." Thus, separation and hierarchy based on skin tone are created, written down, and subsequently spread around.

## 1500s

Post-Spanish and Portuguese colonizers arriving in what would eventually be called North and South America, and said colonizers lumped all the Indigenous (and Brown-skinned) people into one group—"Indians" or *negros da terra* (Blacks from the land). Then a dude named Alonso de Zuazo comes in and contrasts the Black bodies from Africa, said to be "strong for work," and the Brown bodies of the natives, said to be "weak" and able to "work only in undemanding tasks." Voilà! This creates further (completely unfounded) justification for increasing importation of the "strong" enslaved Africans and the ongoing genocide of the "weak" Indigenous peoples. Because, you know, there are lands to overtake and money to be made from them.

## 1700s

Our present-day conception of race becomes a concretely defined thing thanks to a Swedish dude (with a terrible wig, mind you) named Carl Linnaeus. Homie just decides to color-code the "races," attach each to one of the four regions of the world, describe their characteristics, and utilize these characteristics:

- White (*Homo sapiens europaeus*): "Vigorous, muscular. Flowing blond hair. Blue eyes. Very smart, inventive. Covered by tight clothing. Ruled by law."

- Yellow (*Homo sapiens asiaticus*): "Melancholy, stern. Black hair; dark eyes. Strict, haughty, greedy. Covered by loose garments. Ruled by opinion."

- Red (*Homo sapiens americanus*): "Ill-tempered, impassive. Thick straight black hair; wide nostrils; harsh face; beardless. Stubborn, contented, free. Paints himself with red lines. Ruled by custom."

- Black (*Homo sapiens afer*): "Sluggish, lazy. Black kinky hair. Silky skin. Flat nose. Thick lips. Females with genital flap and elongated breasts. Crafty, slow, careless. Covered by grease. Ruled by caprice."

"Race is a power construct . . .
created to give credence to some really
messed-up beliefs and actions held
and committed by a people group—
'fair'-skinned Europeans—who deemed
themselves superior to all others. 'Race'
continues to exist/give and take power/
create interpersonal dynamics because
a long, long time ago, enough people
believed in this claim of superiority
to make it socially true. Then this
*completely unfounded* idea of a human
hierarchy based on a *wholly made-up*
set of criteria spread across the globe.
Unfortunately, with real and lasting
consequences."

Dr. Kendi illustrates the idea of "dueling consciousness" (a term coined by W. E. B. Du Bois in his 1903 work, *The Souls of Black Folk*) using his parents as an example. His parents saw themselves through their own lens of self-determined Black culture, but because they lived in a society where White people set standards based on White superiority, they also had to take on a second set of eyes: those of the White gaze, which set all the rules for any sort of advancement.

## ASSIMILATION

The process of adopting the language, culture, standards, and norms of a dominant social group or nation for the sake of being socially acceptable and integrated.

Dr. Kendi sharpens his focus by saying, "They wanted to liberate but felt the need to assimilate." In the T chart below, consider the differences between liberation and assimilation.

## LIBERATION

Freedom from imprisonment, slavery, or oppressive limitations through the elimination of all ideas and policies that create and perpetuate inequities.

| LIBERATION LOOKS LIKE . . . | ASSIMILATION LOOKS LIKE . . . |
|---|---|
|  |  |
|  |  |
|  |  |
|  |  |

**In what ways might a person of color try to assimilate to White culture? Is this harmful? Why or why not?**

_____

_____

_____

_____

_____

_____

_____

_____

_____

_____

_____

_____

**Do White people struggle with assimilation? Why or why not?**

_____

_____

_____

_____

_____

_____

_____

_____

_____

_____

_____

**What does *liberation* really mean to you? What does it look like for people whose identities are different from yours? For your community, school, or church? Our society at large?**

**Use this space to write about, draw, or collage what liberation <u>looks</u> like to you.**

Review the definitions for **ASSIMILATIONIST** and **SEGREGATIONIST** below. Fill in the Venn diagram opposite with characteristics of segregationists and assimilationists. What are they striving for? Use the middle of the diagram to pin down where they overlap.

## ASSIMILATIONIST

One who expresses the racist idea that a racial group is culturally or behaviorally inferior to the dominant group, and who supports cultural or behavioral enrichment programs to "develop" that racial group up to dominant group standards.

## SEGREGATIONIST

One who expressed the racist idea that a racial group is permanently inferior and can never be developed, and who supports policies that separate that racial group from the "superior" racial group.

ASSIMILATIONIST

SEGREGATIONIST

**Have you ever tried to change something about yourself to fit in? Did it work? Why or why not?**

_____

_____

_____

_____

_____

_____

_____

_____

_____

_____

_____

_____

Many people say certain identifiers—like race or gender—are <u>social constructs</u>, but they're more like <u>power constructs</u>. A power construct is a concept or idea, created by powerful members of society and perpetuated by large-scale acceptance, that exists not in objective reality but as a result of human interaction. Reflect in the space above on what this means to you.

In addition to race and gender, what other power constructs have we built over time? List them here.

"Racist ideas are learned. Basically you hear them over and over again from multiple directions until eventually you believe them and accept them into your worldview—oftentimes without even realizing it (or without realizing some of the things you believe are rooted in racism)."

**Reread the quote on the previous page. If racist ideas are learned, what other destructive ideas have we learned and believed?**

# "Generalizing the actions of racist White individuals to all White people is just as unhelpful and unjustified as generalizing the individual faults and actions of people of color to entire racial groups."

What is your take on this quote? Do you believe generalizations are harmful? Why or why not?

_____

_____

_____

_____

_____

_____

_____

## AS U.S. SUPREME COURT JUSTICE HARRY BLACKMUN

wrote in 1978,

"In order to get beyond racism, we must first take account of race. There is no other way. And in order to treat some persons equally, we must treat them differently."

Based on what you've
learned so far, consider
Harry Blackmun's quote
on the facing page and
jot down your ideas on
how we need to treat
people differently in
order for them to be
treated equally.

**BIOLOGICAL RACISM** is often credited as the foundation of racism. Why do you think this is?

_____

_____

_____

_____

_____

_____

_____

_____

_____

_____

_____

_____

## BIOLOGICAL RACIST IDEA
The idea that the races are meaningfully different in their biology and that these differences create a hierarchy of value.

## BIOLOGICAL ANTIRACIST IDEA
The idea that the races are the same in their biology, and there are no genetic differences that could justify a racial hierarchy.

Make a list of attributes you've heard ascribed to different types of bodies, like Black bodies, White bodies, Asian bodies, Latinx bodies, or Native bodies. Once you've made your list, reread each generalization and label it as either definitively true or false.

1. _____ T ☐ F ☐

2. _____ T ☐ F ☐

3. _____ T ☐ F ☐

4. _____ T ☐ F ☐

5. _____ T ☐ F ☐

6. _____ T ☐ F ☐

Why did you label each idea on the previous page as true
or false? How can you tell if generalizations are rooted
in truth?

_____

_____

_____

_____

_____

_____

_____

_____

_____

_____

"THIS IS ONE OF THE GREAT DANGERS OF *NOT* DELIBERATELY PURSUING ANTIRACISM. SAYING AND/OR DOING NOTHING ALLOWS *MULTIPLE* SYSTEMS OF OPPRESSION TO THRIVE."

"Bodily antiracism means doing away with the (racist) idea that certain bodies—especially Black ones—are dangerous by virtue of their existence. It means not viewing relatively high violent crime levels in low-income Black neighborhoods as confirmation or evidence that Black people are innately more violent."

**Based on the definition below, or what you might have read in** *How to Be a (Young) Antiracist,* **what are some potential examples of BODILY RACIST IDEAS?**

## BODILY RACIST IDEAS

The belief that certain racialized bodies are more animal-like and prone to violence than others.

**Has anyone ever ascribed certain actions or abilities to your body? Actions or abilities that you know are not true or that you are simply not interested in?**

_____

_____

_____

_____

_____

_____

_____

_____

_____

_____

_____

What are some stereotypes you've heard about a race/gender/
orientation/class group you belong to (whether negative or
positive) that just don't fit who you are? Write them down here:

Now rip this page out,
crumple or tear it up,
and throw it away.

# What do you know about <u>INTERSECTIONALITY?</u>

USE YOUR OWN WORDS TO DEFINE IT HERE.

**INTERSECTIONALITY:** The interconnected nature of social categorizations—e.g., race, gender, class, orientation, ethnicity—as they apply to any given individual or group, creating the experience of overlapping systems of oppression.

In *How to Be a (Young) Antiracist*, the authors split their book into sections based on the facets of human identity. Two straight Black folks may identify with each other based on their Blackness and straightness, but may not identify with each other based on their class, gender, or ethnicity.

Use the grid below to list the many ways in which race, gender, orientation, and so on can show up in a person's identity. Consider all gender expressions, ethnicities, and any other identifiers that feel important to you, like disability, immigration status, health diagnoses, hair type, or anything else not included here.

| RACE | GENDER | ORIENTATION | ETHNICITY | CLASS | OTHER |
|---|---|---|---|---|---|
| | | | | | |
| | | | | | |
| | | | | | |
| | | | | | |
| | | | | | |
| | | | | | |

Use your identity lists to explore your own identity. How do you identify? Then come up with as many identity combinations as you can.

Here are a few to get you started:

**Light-skinned cisgender straight Black man**

**Middle-class nonbinary White lesbian**

**Southeast Asian American transgender man**

Use the Venn diagram below to consider the differences between **RACE-ORIENTATIONS**. Use one circle for a relationship between a cis man and cis woman of the same race, and another circle for a relationship between queer people of the same race.

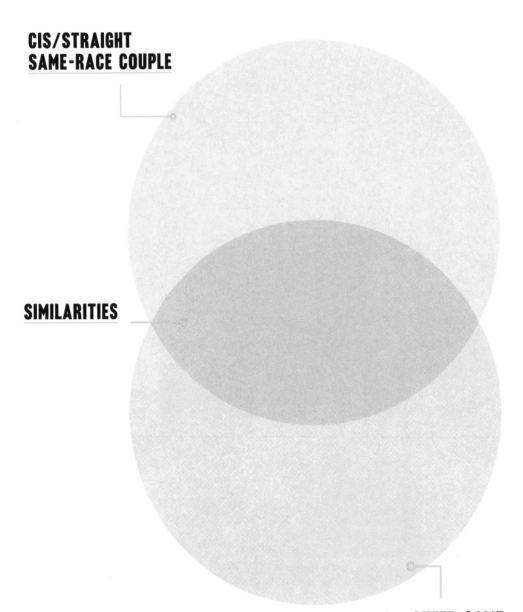

**CIS/STRAIGHT SAME-RACE COUPLE**

**SIMILARITIES**

**QUEER SAME-RACE COUPLE**

**Consider the differences between the two couples. What rights do they have access to? How are they allowed or expected to behave in public? Do you think this is fair? Explain.**

Can you think of (or research!) an example of a race- and gender-based policy that might lead to unequal outcomes for different groups of people?

Here's an example answer to get you thinking: gendered racial wage gaps

"Like gender racism, queer racism also has to be uprooted in order for one to be truly antiracist. Opposing racism but failing/refusing to address queerphobia completely undermines all attempts at antiracism because ignoring policies that negatively impact queer people means allowing inequities between race-orlentations—and therefore inequities between racial groups—to endure. . . . *Whole* people must be accepted wholly."

# Draw a flowchart of an example of a CLASS-RACIST policy that might create the effects that are then attributed to a person's RACE-CLASS.

Here's an example to get you started:

REDLINING IN THE 1930s →

PROPERTY VALUATIONS OF BLACK HOMES AND NEIGHBORHOODS FALL

↓

THE GOVERNMENT CONTINUES POLICIES THAT ENSURE DISINVESTMENT IN BLACK COMMUNITIES

←

BLACK PEOPLE ARE FALSELY BLAMED FOR "NOT CARING" ABOUT THEIR HOMES AND NEIGHBORHOODS

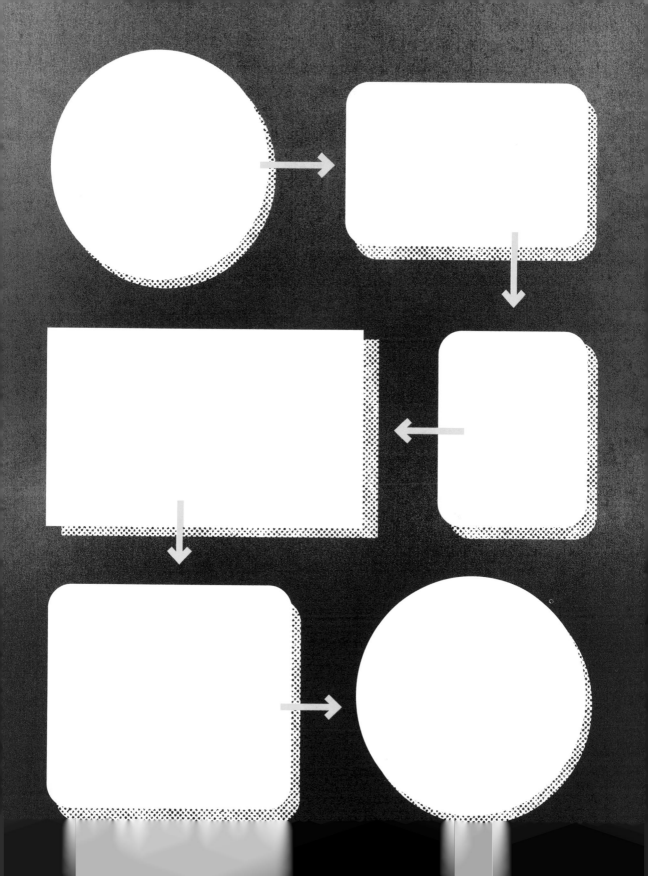

Similar to young Ibram's love of "The Ave" (the culturally vibrant intersection of Jamaica Avenue and 164th Street in Queens, New York), what's a place in your hometown that you love? Describe or draw what you see, smell, hear, taste, touch, and do there for someone who has never been.

"Collective subjectivity is the source of _RACIST POWER_. Enough people of European descent agreed that their way of life was *the* Way of Life, and deemed any *other* way of life not only inferior, but subhuman. To drive this idea home, some of them enslaved individuals from cultural and ethnic backgrounds that didn't meet the standard, and then spread the word of those groups' inferiority . . . which, by default, further strengthened the idea of European superiority, and European culture/traditions/thoughts/ideas as the ideal everyone should ascribe to.

Which means that when spaces *aren't* governed by this so-called 'universal standard,' especially here in these United States, those spaces are seen as suspect (or even deviant, depending on who you're talking to)."

# Food for thought: Let's debunk some of the racist ideas about Black culture.

Debunking can be applied to all iterations of **CULTURAL RACISM**. For instance:

**1.** **LANGUAGE.** There is no *correct* English. Language is a human creation designed for ease of communication and transmission of meaning, and it is *constantly* changing. In other words, *we* are the masters of language, not the other way around. *We* determine how language is used and what form it takes in our everyday lives, and it is *entirely normal* for those uses and forms to vary based on where we are, who we're talking to, and what we're talking about and in what format (e.g., spoken, written, or communicated with our hands, as in sign language). The best part: If the person you're communicating with understands what you're expressing, you have communicated effectively. Full stop.

**2.** **STYLE.** There is no *inferior* or *universally proper* or *moral* way to dress. Like language, fashion is a human creation used for self-expression and/or *intra*cultural conveyance of meaning. Examples: the hijab, a headscarf worn by many Muslim women, or the *dastār*, a turban worn by Sikh men.

**3.** **MUSIC.** Same as the first two, music is a human creation. There is no "right" or "wrong." There is personal preference, of course—you prefer hip-hop to death metal, for instance—but all music is enjoyable to *someone*. And that's all that matters.

There's no *incorrect* expression of faith or emotions or a *standard* way to interact with other members of your cultural group. No culture is *better* or *more civilized* than any other culture. And there is, therefore, no need to assimilate to meet some imaginary *proper* cultural ideal.

# Think of the first time you saw something from your culture represented in American culture, however you define it.

Was the representation respectful? Why or why not?

_____

_____

_____

If you see your culture represented within American culture all the time, how does that make you feel?

_____

_____

_____

Do you think people you know from other cultures see themselves represented?

_____

_____

_____

Do you have a sibling or cousin or friend who shares your culture, but is of a different gender than you? Have you ever noticed that different expectations of behaviors or roles are applied to you both?

ME

SIMILARITIES

SIBLING/
COUSIN/FRIEND

Draw a Venn diagram with
one circle for you and the
behaviors expected of your
gender, and another circle for
your sibling/cousin/friend and
the behaviors expected of their
gender, with the overlapping
part for what's expected of both
of you. What do you notice?

# QUICK HISTORY: The War on Drugs

Okay, so all of this stuff might still feel pretty philosophical, right? You might wonder how racism has affected Americans over the past, say, 50 years . . . so, let's look at the late 1960s to start—after Martin Luther King Jr.'s assassination, in the midst of the 20-year-long Vietnam War, and during the rise of the Black power and women's liberation movements.

In **1965**, President Lyndon B. Johnson declared it "the year when this country began a thorough, intelligent, and effective war on crime." This statement alone is not a big deal, but there were a whooooooole lot of pervasive racist ideas floating around at that point . . . including ones about which demographic of people was committing the most crime.

President Johnson's **1960s** war on crime morphed into President Nixon's **1970s** war on drugs, which President Reagan doubled down on in the 1980s by employing "stronger law enforcement," harsher penalties for drug crimes, and mandatory sentencing. The effects of these policies *definitely* created a smorgasbord of racial inequities that have yet to be corrected literally half a century later.

As a result of these harsh policies and "stronger law enforcement"—*not* because there was more crime, mind you—the American prison population *quadrupled* between **1980 AND 2000**. It didn't make a ton of sense: Black and Latinx people wound up *wildly* overrepresented in the prison population—they made up 56 percent of prisoners despite being only 31 percent of the overall population—even though drug use rates are about the same across Black, Latinx, and White communities.

If you thought the glaring racial inequity in drug arrest numbers compared to drug use statistics was bad, think about what happens when those arrest numbers are viewed through the lens of racist ideas. The very nature of racist ideas is that they root the disparities in people, not policy. Which means people assumed—and still assume—that more Black people getting arrested for drug offenses is "proof" that more Black people use and sell drugs . . . aka "proof" that there's something inherently wrong with Black people.

Food for thought: Read the history
lesson on the previous page.
Consider the last racist thought you
had or heard—either about your
own race or someone else's. Have
you ever considered the effect a
single thought may have on your
view of an entire race? This is
how sneaky racism can be.

**How does the word *racist* feel when you hear or say it?
Is it a weapon or a descriptor? Why?**

1. The (*false*) statement "Black girls and
   Latinas are more promiscuous" is a form of a
   _____ racist idea.


2. When a person believes racist ideas about
   their own race, this is an example of a
   _____ racist idea.


3. The (*false*) statement "Black people have
   'more natural physical ability'" is an
   example of _____ racism.


4. Microaggressions—aka insults,
   invalidations, assaults—may also be
   called _____, because
   _____ more accurately
   describes the actions and their effects on
   people: confusion, distress, anger, worry,

depression, anxiety, fatigue, and
sometimes suicide.

5. Heavier policing of low-income areas mostly
   populated by Black people than of middle-
   and upper-class areas full of White people
   is an example of _____
   _____ at work.

Phew, that was *a lot*. How are you doing? Is anything really puzzling you at this moment? Is there anything that gave you a light-bulb moment? Jot it down here and come back to this page whenever you want to remember something major. (Dog-ear the page or flag it with a sticky note, too, so you remember there are important notes here!)

# PAUSE TO CHECK IN WITH YOURSELF.

❋ Unclench your jaw, relax your shoulders, get some fresh air.

❋ How are you feeling?

❋ Drink some water or have a snack.

❋ Talk to a trusted friend or family member.

❋ Write down how you feel.

❋ Give yourself a pat on the back (yes, seriously!) for committing to this hard work.

# REFLECT

Now that we've covered *a lot* of that good, good research from *How to Be a (Young) Antiracist*, this section will ask some more personal questions about your experiences and the experiences of those around you. This is your space to reflect on the ways race and racism are present in your daily life. Your awareness is key—mindfulness of your surroundings, your own thoughts and actions, the way you speak about others— this is all part of what will unlock positive antiracist change.

**We'll start this reflection section with some easy questions about your experiences—questions about *you!***

## 20 QUESTIONS TO GET TO KNOW ME

1. Favorite childhood memory: _____

2. Biggest life goal: _____

3. Best personality trait: _____

4. Favorite teacher: _____

5. Favorite musical artist: _____

6. Favorite song: _____

7. Favorite TV show: _____

8. Favorite movie: _____

9. Favorite book: _____

10. Pet peeve: _____

11. Favorite family or cultural tradition: _____

12. Favorite meal to eat: _____

13. Favorite meal to cook: _____

14. Most memorable trip/vacation: _____

15. Languages I speak: _____

16. Best stress reliever: _____

17. Favorite emotion: _____

18. Favorite place: _____

19. Zodiac sign: _____

20. Favorite restaurant: _____

Why is it important to develop your own identity? How do you feel about people whose identities look totally different from yours? What emotions show up when you encounter someone who looks/acts/sounds/expresses themselves differently than you do?

**Think of your cultural background within your racial identity; list some things/practices that make your cultural background unique.**

2

**Now think of someone you know with a cultural background that is different than yours; list some things/practices that make their cultural background unique.**

_____

_____

_____

_____

_____

_____

_____

_____

_____

_____

_____        (See, it's totally possible to
                                          appreciate each other's unique
                                          cultures without treating each
_____         other differently!)

**FOOD FOR THOUGHT:** Racist power is often very good at spreading racist ideas like wildfire. And folks of any race are susceptible to believing and internalizing these racist ideas about their own race without knowing it. This is called <u>INTERNALIZED RACISM.</u>

What other judgments, beliefs, or straight-up hateful ideas have *you* internalized about yourself? Where did they come from?

Have you ever believed stereotypes about a person who was a member of a marginalized race/gender/orientation/class group? What did you believe and why? How did you realize it was a mistaken belief? Was this an example of **CONFIRMATION BIAS** or **INTERNALIZED OPPRESSION?**

**CONFIRMATION BIAS:** The tendency to interpret, recall, and/or search for information in a way that supports one's existing beliefs.

**INTERNALIZED OPPRESSION:** When members of a marginalized group accept and/or reaffirm negative stereotypes against their own group and come to believe and/or act as though the belief system, values, and way of life of the dominant group are correct.

**What might be an example of internalized oppression you've seen in your own family or community?**

Here's an example answer to get you thinking: Black and Latinx kids don't expect to do well on tests...which then causes test anxiety that would prevent anyone from doing well on a test. (This particular iteration of internalized oppression actually has a name: *stereotype threat*.)

**Think of a person you've crushed on (whether in a romantic way or an I-really-*really*-want-to-be-friends-with-that-person type of way). Now imagine that all the messages you receive made you think that it was wrong or abnormal to like this person. How would you feel?**

_____

_____

_____

_____

_____

_____

_____

_____

_____

_____

_____

Imagine Racism as a dastardly villain ravaging your community, sabotaging antiracist efforts, and stealing from your neighbors.

What does Racism look like?

What are its powers?

1.

2.

3.

Write a character study of Racism and its personality traits.

Or, draw a portrait of Racism, labeling its
skills and the powers of its villain costume.

As long as racism has been a thing, White spaces have been considered not only superior, but universal: the "standard" for how all spaces should operate.

## THIS IS THE CRUX OF SPACE RACISM.

Often, spaces filled with Black (and sometimes brown) bodies aren't "governed by Black people, Black thoughts, Black cultures, Black histories, nor Black traditions. In fact, the guiding principles in *every* educational space you attended prior to undergrad were governed by Whiteness: White thoughts, White ideas of what constitutes right and wrong, White histories, White traditions, White teachers and administrators. So in these very Black-*looking* spaces, you and everyone around you was expected to live up to White-space standards."

Think about the spaces you interact with in your regular life. Do you usually have to adjust to a whole different set of ideas, norms, and a code of conduct from what you might be used to at home?

_____

_____

_____

_____

If yes, imagine what your ideal space would be like—what histories and ideas would be talked about, what traditions or practices might be adhered to? If no, what about the spaces you interact with feels like home to you? Can you see how certain norms might alienate others?

_____

_____

_____

_____

"Is borrowing elements of other people's cultures a crime? Of course not. . . . what tends to bother people of color about this 'borrowing' is that it's a one-way street; only members of the dominant culture can cherry-pick which elements they want to 'borrow' from marginalized cultures and which cultural elements will be a source of continued marginalization. The same person who decides to wear cornrows like yours might feel threatened and pull out a gun if they see you wearing a hoodie.

At the end of the day, the most important thing to reflect upon is this: Being antiracist does involve respectfully enjoying and appreciating the cultures of other racialized groups . . . but that appreciation must involve the *totality* of cultures to truly be antiracist. Deciding to appreciate some aspects of another group's culture while rejecting or denouncing other aspects misses the mark."

Research the history of a trend from a culture that is different from yours. Draw a picture of the hairstyle, type of music, piece of clothing, or whatever it is here.

Label it with three interesting facts you learned from your research.

1.

2.

3.

Is there a difference between appropriating phrases from cultural groups different than yours and **LINGUISTIC REAPPROPRIATION** that happens within that cultural group? Share your thoughts here.

_____

_____

_____

_____

_____

_____

_____

_____

_____

_____

## LINGUISTIC REAPPROPRIATION:

The cultural process by which a group reclaims words or language historically used to demean or disparage, creating semantic change that neutralizes the words over time.

_____

_____

_____

Can you think of some phrases or actions that are considered benign when White people say or do them but are sources of disdain when said or done by a person whose culture the phrase or action comes from?

_____

_____

_____

_____

_____

_____

_____

_____

_____

_____

_____

"BEING ANTIRACIST INVOLVES *COMPLETELY* ELIMINATING ANY BEAUTY STANDARD THAT ELEVATES A PARTICULAR SKIN OR EYE COLOR, HAIR TEXTURE, FACIAL FEATURE, OR BODY TYPE SHARED BY ANY ONE PARTICULAR GROUP. IT MEANS DIVERSIFYING OUR STANDARDS AND SEEING *ALL* NATURAL BEAUTY— THAT'S PHYSICAL APPEARANCE WITHOUT *ANY* ALTERATIONS OR ENHANCEMENTS—AS EQUAL."

# What is your personal definition of *beauty*?

## 1955: MONTGOMERY BUS BOYCOTT

*Montgomery, Alabama*

In December of 1955, a Black woman named Rosa Parks refused to give up her seat to a White person, sparking one of the most prominent civil rights protests in American history. The Montgomery bus boycott officially began four days after Parks's arrest and lasted for one year and sixteen days, ending in a U.S. Supreme Court decision that declared the Alabama and Montgomery laws that segregated buses unconstitutional.

## 1960: THE SIT-IN MOVEMENT

*Greensboro, North Carolina, and beyond*

In 1960, four Black students at North Carolina Agricultural and Technical State University, inspired by Dr. Martin Luther King Jr.'s practice of nonviolent protest, decided to act against the segregationist policies of department store F. W. Woolworth. When the Greensboro Four (as they would soon be known) were refused service at the segregated lunch counter designated for White customers, they simply sat quietly at the counter until the store closed that night. Over the next few days, the Greensboro Four recruited hundreds of protestors to join them and sit-ins soon began happening all over the South—in Virginia, Kentucky, Tennessee, Mississippi, and beyond. Dozens of sit-ins that year would prove the power of unity, collective action, and nonviolent protest.

## 1961: THE FREEDOM RIDES

*Alabama, South Carolina, and beyond*

Despite the U.S. Supreme Court decisions that ruled the segregation of public buses and interstate bus terminals unconstitutional, many people in power in the American South continued to enforce segregation in the 1950s and '60s. In 1961, as a form of protest, groups of Black and White civil rights activists (including a young John Lewis, who would go on to serve in the U.S. House of Representatives from 1986 until his death in 2020) began taking Freedom Rides through Southern states, challenging the segregated status quo. These buses full of activists provoked violent reactions from supporters of segregation, drew national attention to the civil rights movement, and eventually resulted in a ripple effect of positive policy change.

Did you learn about these events in school? How do you think a major protest like these might shape a social justice movement?

**Let's get quizzical! And by that, we mean: Take a look at the questions below and do your best to answer them correctly. If you need help, ask a friend or family member to discuss with you.**

1. Label each of the following statements as true or false.

   a) Colorism is exclusive to the Black community.

   b) "White flight" (aka the large-scale migration of White people out of areas that are becoming more racially and/or ethnically diverse) is often related to bodily racism.

   c) Most race-related fear—especially of Black, Latinx, and Arab people—is proportionate to actual violence carried out by individuals from these backgrounds.

   d) Anyone (regardless of race) can perpetuate racial inequities by aligning themselves with racist power through unchecked racist ideas.

   e) "Whiteness" is a power construct created by human actions and beliefs that has generated power differences among groups of people.

2. What physical factors might determine how a person and their ethnic group is racialized? Meaning, what factors superficially establish a person's race?

   a) Height, weight, and body shape

   b) Skin tone and hair texture

   c) Accent, language, and personal style

   d) All of the above

3. Policies that create inequitable living conditions for poor people of color are examples of

    a) gender racism

    b) colorism

    c) cultural racism

    d) class racism

4. The real reason for inequality between White and non-White schools (like many other racial inequities) comes down to

    a) economic racial injustices and an unequal distribution of resources

    b) the cultural differences between White and non-White students

    c) the makeup of the administration at each type of school

    d) colorism

5. "Being and looking more like White people, Chinese or Korean people are smarter and more attractive than people of Indian or Pakistani descent." This is an example of what racism combo?

    a) ethnic and bodily racism

    b) cultural and ethnic racism

    c) cultural and class racism

    d) bodily and behavioral racism

In *How to Be a (Young) Antiracist,* the authors use two metaphors to illustrate the insidious nature of racism.

Using your understanding of racism, read the prompts on each page and flesh out each metaphor, drawing its many parts and labeling what each part of your drawing represents.

Consider racism as a tree with bountiful fruit and deep roots. Consider what each part of the tree represents, from its physical presence to the ways it contributes to its surrounding environment. Is it possible to cut this tree down?

Envision racism
as a fierce boxer
approaching you for a
fight. What shape does
this "boxer" take?
What does it wear
for protection? How
does it move? What
blows can you strike
against it? Can it
be defeated?

"WE'RE PRODUCTS OF OUR ENVIRONMENT. BECAUSE, AS YOU'LL LEARN, THE STATUS QUO—THE EXISTING SOCIETAL STRUCTURE REGARDING SOCIAL OR POLITICAL ISSUES—

IS A VERY REAL THING. AND UNLESS WE PAUSE TO EXAMINE IT, AND THEN CHALLENGE ITS FLAWS, IT ROLLS ON, THRIVING ON OUR IGNORANCE AND SILENCE."

**What are some problematic ideas or norms that you've been able to move away from? How and when did you realize something didn't feel right?**

**How can you challenge the status quo? What can you do today? In what *big* way might you disrupt the status quo?**

# PAUSE TO CHECK IN WITH YOURSELF.

* Unclench your jaw, relax your shoulders, get some fresh air.

* How are you feeling?

* Drink some water or have a snack.

* Talk to a trusted friend or family member.

* Write down how you feel.

* Give yourself a pat on the back (yes, seriously!) for committing to this hard work.

ACT

"EARLY IN LIFE, I HAD LEARNED
THAT IF YOU WANT SOMETHING, YOU
HAD BETTER MAKE SOME NOISE."
—MALCOLM X

This section is all about *action*. There is
no catchall method for dealing with racism,
but it's important to remember that any
action—big or small—can have a positive
ripple effect on those around you. You're
going to interact with a lot of people in
your lifetime—some of whom you can
enlighten or change, some of whom will
not budge from racist beliefs—and your
antiracist actions will depend on the
situations you find yourself in.

The exercises in this section will prep
you for these kinds of interactions. It's
important to be knowledgeable, flexible,
and compassionate—not only to others,
but to yourself, too. This stuff is
hard work.

**SO WHAT NOW?** What action can you take? Well, the short answer is: It depends. The longer answer is: There is no one-size-fits-all, take-these-steps-to-change-the-world action plan for changemaking.

That said . . . what you can do is get yourself ready to act.

Think of it like training to become a firefighter. It's impossible to predict how, when, and where blazes will break out, but a set of adaptable basic skills enable firefighters to fight—and usually put out—just about any fire.

Let's tuck four final definitions into that glorious brain of yours. And to keep it simple (and hopefully easy-ish to remember), like the word *changemaker*, they all begin with C.

**COGENCY** The state or quality of being clear, logical, and convincing.

**COMPASSION** Sympathetic concern for the sufferings of others.

**CREATIVITY** The ability to transcend traditional ideas, rules, patterns, or relationships and create meaningful new ideas, forms, methods, and/or interpretations.

**COLLABORATION** The process of two or more people, groups, or entities working in tandem to complete a task, produce a product, or achieve a goal.

**BRAINSTORM A LIST OF YOUR SUPERPOWERS.** This list can include anything from your talent for graphic design to your ability to talk to anyone about anything. It can include physical assets and emotional strengths. Think about what you have to offer the world, and even if you don't know what you'll use them for yet, list your superpowers here.

- _____

- _____

- _____

- _____

- _____

- _____

- _____

- _____

- _____

- _____

- _____

Match your superpowers with folks in your community (IRL or online) that you might be able to influence—whether it's through educational tweets for like-minded friends, a stern conversation with your uncle about not using slurs, or a productive chat with a local politician.

**SUPERPOWERS**                    **PEOPLE TO INFLUENCE**

**What is your favorite social media platform? Social media can be a great place to start conversations about antiracism, raise money for local organizations, recruit volunteers for community efforts, or share interesting facts about other changemakers your age.**

## CHOOSE A PLATFORM (CIRCLE ONE):

Instagram    Twitter    TikTok    Snapchat    YouTube    Other

## CHOOSE A TYPE OF POST:

- Research a specific holiday (e.g., Martin Luther King Jr. Day, Earth Day, Thanksgiving) and provide an intersectional overview of what you learn. Are there certain important figures that history glosses over? Is our collective understanding of this holiday missing the big picture? Share your post on the holiday to raise awareness of your findings.

- Make a video of your top five favorite things about your culture to share with friends and followers. It can be anything from your grandma's favorite dessert to a specific hairstyle you remember from your childhood. Sharing your culture is a way to celebrate our world's diversity.

- Watch a television show with a protagonist whose race is different than yours. Share your favorite quotes, screencaps, or OMG-I-wish-they'd-just-date-already! moments from the show on social media.

- Look online for an organization that tackles a specific type of racism you learned about from this workbook (e.g., class racism, gender racism, space racism). Find out what kind of donations the organization takes and share this knowledge with your friends, family, and followers online. Encourage people to make their own donations and keep track of how much money your community raises.

- Use your platform to start an antiracist book club. Share favorite passages and quotes, give a summary of what you learned, discuss the content live, or make a piece of art to share inspired by the book.

Changemakers are often faced with tough conversations. Fighting for an antiracist future does not come without its speed bumps. What kinds of conversations are easy for you to have? Which ones are the hardest?

Consider a recent conversation about race you wish you'd handled differently. Pretend you get a do-over. Rewrite your exchange as if it were happening via text message:

# WHAT IS CIVIC ENGAGEMENT?

A lot of folks will tell you that voting is the single most important superpower you have as an American citizen, but civic engagement goes way beyond electoral politics. On a national scale, the United States' annual elections are a crucial part of your civic duty. And it doesn't stop there.

According to youth.gov, a U.S. government website focused on building community through youth-serving programs, *youth civic engagement* is defined as working to make a difference in the civic life of one's community.

What does that mean for you? What kinds of things could use improving in your community—from adding a stop sign at a dangerous intersection to fundraising for your local antiracist organizations? Dream up a wish list of improvements for your community on the facing page and reflect on how you might contribute to one of these causes on the following spread.

- 

---

- 

---

- 

---

- 

---

- 

---

- 

---

- 

---

- 

---

- 

---

- 

---

- 

---

- 

---

- 

---

-

**MY NEXT CIVIC STEPS:** So, you have big dreams, huh? Good! Now's the time to slow it down and make small, incremental (aka *doable!*) steps toward that big, pie-in-the-sky dream of creating a community art center or starting an antiracism newsletter or whatever you've dreamt up on the previous page.

Choose a dream to pursue and break it down into small, measurable actions. Consider each action a "level up" moment that gets you closer to your goal. Think about the help you'll need to enlist, the people you'll introduce yourself to, the types of resources you'll require, how you'll spread your message, and how you'll have fun while doing it! Working with your community can be super fulfilling, so make sure to add some creative, fun steps to your process.

DREAM

6.

5.

4.

3.

2.

1.

After you've mapped out your steps, research what's going on in your community. Are there organizations you can tap for help? Are there bills or policies in the works to support your efforts? Can you get your school, library, or local pizza shop to help? Use this page to take notes on how to make your dream happen.

**Art is a powerful way to express yourself politically, whether it's through writing a protest poem or painting a Black Lives Matter mural for a local community center.**

**Here are some ideas for creating your own art. Grab some paper, a pencil or paintbrush, or a camera and make something . . . anything!**

- Write a poem or rap about a headline from today's news.

- Design a graphic to share on social media that educates your followers about a policy that needs to change or a politician you support.

- Create a vision board based on one of these prompts:

  - What does a racially just future look like?

  - What does *beauty* mean to you? What does it look like?

  - What does *culture* mean to you? Celebrate it!

- Listen to an audiobook that centers on race and/or antiracism and paint while you listen.

**What kind of protests or community events could you attend? Make a list. If they don't exist yet, add 'em anyway and dream with some friends about how you can make them happen!**

- _____

- _____

- _____

- _____

- _____

- _____

- _____

- _____

- _____

- _____

- _____

- _____

- _____

# EXPRESS YOURSELF!

Use the next few pages to create your own antiracist posters. Decorate a poster with powerful quotes or a list of reasons to fight for change. Design a protest poster to bring to a local march or demonstration. Create something affirmative for a friend or share a favorite antiracist quote with a family member. Use these posters however will best support your antiracist actions.

"A SHIFT IN
A SINGLE
PERSPECTIVE
CAN BE AN
EXCEEDINGLY
POWERFUL THING."

-NIC STONE

**What do you know about mission statements? Dr. Kendi developed a manifesto of sorts, listing out a plan to guide his work. This mission statement helped shape his goals when he founded the Boston University Center for Antiracist Research:**

- Admit racial inequity is a problem of bad policy, not bad people.
- Identify racial inequity in all its intersections and manifestations.
- Investigate and uncover the racist policies causing racial inequity.
- Invent or find antiracist policy that can eliminate racial inequity.
- Figure out who or what group has the power to institute antiracist policy.
- Disseminate and educate about the uncovered racist policy and antiracist policy correctives.
- Work with antiracist policymakers to institute the antiracist policy.
- Deploy antiracist power to compel or drive from power the racist policymakers to institute the antiracist policy.
- Monitor closely to ensure the antiracist policy reduces and eliminates racial inequity.
- When policies fail, do not blame the people. Start over and seek out new and more effective antiracist treatments until they work.
- Monitor closely to prevent new racist policies from being instituted.

Using Dr. Kendi's list of antiracist missions, use the next page to write out your own antiracist missions. They can either be things to remember or goals to work toward. Then, tear out the page and tuck it in a binder or hang it up in your room to remind you of your importance while doing this work.

# A MANIFESTO

GRAND SCALE CHANGEMAKING ISN'T
ONLY POSSIBLE, IT'S *TRULY* WITHIN
REACH. FIND SOME PEOPLE WHO FEEL
THE SAME WAY ABOUT STUFF THAT
YOU DO. THEN, DRIVEN BY SHARED
COMPASSION, COME TOGETHER TO
CREATE A COGENT EXPLANATION
OF YOUR POSITION AND MISSION,
COMBINE YOUR VARIED STRENGTHS
AND AREAS OF EXPERTISE, AND
COLLABORATE TO CARRY IT OUT.
LET'S GET IT.

# GLOSSARY

**RACISM:** A powerful collection of **policies** that sustains **racial inequities** and is substantiated by ideas of racial hierarchy. Also known as *institutional racism, structural racism*, and *systemic racism*.

**RACIST** (adjective): In support of a **racist policy** through actions or inaction, or expressing a **racist idea**, both of which produce and normalize **racial inequities**.

**RACIAL INEQUITY:** When two or more racial groups are not standing on relatively equal footing.

**POLICY:** Written and unwritten laws, rules, procedures, processes, regulations, and guidelines that govern people.

**RACIST POLICY:** Any **policy** that produces or sustains **racial inequity** among racial groups.

**RACIST POWER: Racist** policymakers creating and upholding policies that sustain racial inequities.

**RACIST IDEA:** Any idea that suggests one racial group is inferior or superior to another racial group in any way.

**ANTIRACISM:** A powerful collection of **policies** that lead to **racial equity** and are substantiated by ideas of racial equality.

**ANTIRACIST** (adjective): In support of an **antiracist policy** through actions or inaction, or expressing an **antiracist idea**, both of which produce and normalize **racial equity**.

**ANTIRACIST** (noun): One who makes the conscious decision to support or enact policies and expresses ideas that produce and normalize racial equity, while denouncing, pointing out, and standing against policies and ideas that sustain racial inequity.

**RACIAL EQUITY:** When two or more racial groups are standing on relatively equal footing and experience relatively similar and/or equal outcomes.

**ANTIRACIST POLICY:** Any **policy** that produces or sustains **racial equity** among racial groups.

**ANTIRACIST IDEA:** Any idea that suggests that all racial groups are equals, that there is no racial group that is superior or inferior to any other racial group.

**DISCRIMINATION:** Treating, considering, or making a distinction in favor or against a person or people group based on group, class, or category.

**RACIST DISCRIMINATION:** Discrimination based on a person's or people group's race that creates and/or perpetuates **racial inequity**.

**ANTIRACIST DISCRIMINATION:** Discrimination based on a person's or people group's race that creates **racial equity**.

**LIBERATION:** Freedom from imprisonment, slavery, or oppressive limitations through the elimination of all ideas and **policies** that create and perpetuate **inequities**.

**SEGREGATIONIST:** One who expresses the **racist idea** that a racial group is permanently inferior and can never be developed, and who supports **policies** that separate that racial group from the perceived superior racial group.

**ASSIMILATIONIST:** One who expresses the **racist idea** that a racial group is culturally or behaviorally inferior to the dominant group, and who supports cultural or behavioral enrichment programs to "develop" that racial group up to dominant group standards.

**ANTIRACIST:** One who expresses the idea that racial groups are equals in every way and that none needs developing, and who supports **policy** that reduces **racial inequity**.

# POWER

**RACE:** A socially sustained **power construct** created to separate and define collections of people based on observable, shared characteristics.

**POWER CONSTRUCT:** A concept or idea, created by powerful members of society and perpetuated by large-scale acceptance, that exists not in objective reality but as a result of human interaction.

# BIOLOGY

**BIOLOGICAL RACIST IDEA:** The idea that the races are meaningfully different in their biology and that these differences create a hierarchy of value.

**BIOLOGICAL ANTIRACIST IDEA:** The idea that the races are the same in their biology and there are no genetic differences that could justify a racial hierarchy.

# BEHAVIOR

**BEHAVIORAL RACIST IDEA:** Making individuals responsible for the perceived behavior of racial groups and making racial group membership responsible for the behavior of individuals.

**BEHAVIORAL ANTIRACISM:** Eliminating the idea of racial group behavior and seeing individuals as responsible for their individual choices and actions regardless of their race.

# BLACK

**INTERNALIZED RACISM:** Ascribing to **racist ideas** and supporting **racist policies** that contribute to **racial inequities** that negatively impact one's own racial group.

**SLUR:** A disparaging remark or slight aimed at a member or members of a particular group, typically used to intimidate and/or remind said group member(s) of their marginalization on a societal level.

**LINGUISTIC REAPPROPRIATION:** The cultural process by which a group reclaims words or language historically used to demean or disparage, creating semantic change that neutralizes the words over time.

# WHITE

**WHITE SUPREMACY:** The belief, theory, or doctrine that White people are inherently superior to people from all other racial and ethnic groups, and are therefore rightfully the dominant group in any society.

# COLOR

**COLORISM:** A form of prejudice and/or **racist discrimination** in which people of the same racial or ethnic group are treated differently based on skin color both by fellow group members and individuals of other racial and ethnic backgrounds.

# ETHNICITY

**ETHNICITY:** The sharing of a common and distinctive culture, language, religion, national origin, and/or set of physical features among a group of people.

# BODY

**BODILY RACISM:** The belief that certain racialized bodies are more animal-like and prone to violence than others.

**CONFIRMATION BIAS:** The tendency to interpret, recall, and/or search for information in a way that supports one's existing beliefs.

# GENDER

**INTERSECTIONALITY:** The interconnected nature of social categorizations—e.g., race, gender, class, orientation, ethnicity—as they apply to any given individual or group, creating the experience of overlapping systems of discrimination.

**RACE-GENDER:** The single identity marker created by combining an individual or group's race and gender identity (e.g., Black woman; White men; Latinx trans woman; Asian nonbinary people).

**GENDER RACISM:** A powerful collection of **racist policies**, substantiated by **racist ideas**, that lead to inequity among race-genders.

# ORIENTATION

**RACE-ORIENTATION:** The single identity marker created by combining racial group membership and orientation (e.g., Kaila is a Black lesbian).

**QUEER RACISM:** A powerful collection of **racist policies**, substantiated by **racist ideas**, that lead to inequity among **race-orientations**.

**INTERNALIZED OPPRESSION:** When members of a marginalized group accept and/or reaffirm negative stereotypes against their own group and come to believe and/or act as though the belief system, values, and way of life of the dominant group are correct.

**TOKENISM:** A forced form of diversity that involves including, recruiting, or hiring a small number of people from underrepresented groups to create the superficial appearance of equity or equality.

# CLASS

**RACE-CLASS:** A grouping of people at the intersection of race and class (e.g., the Native poor; Black elites; White middle class).

**CLASS RACISM:** The support of **policies** of racial capitalism against members of specific **race-classes**, and attempting to justify **racial inequities** among race-classes with **racist ideas**.

## CULTURE

**CULTURE:** The sum total way of life, including shared beliefs, behaviors, customs, and art forms, built up by a group of people and transmitted from one generation to another.

**CULTURAL RACISM:** The imposition of a cultural standard, conceived and perpetuated by racist power through **racist ideas**, that creates a cultural hierarchy among racial groups.

**CULTURAL ANTIRACIST:** One who rejects the notion of a cultural ideal and sees all cultures of all racial groups as equal and valid.

**CULTURAL APPROPRIATION:** The act of adopting or taking possession of cultural identity markers, including language, traditions, and/or style, from minority communities without permission or acknowledgment, and often in ways that garner profit for members of the dominant culture.

## SPACE

**SPACE RACISM:** A powerful collection of **racist policies**, supported by **racist ideas**, that leads to unequal resources in racialized spaces and/or disdain for or dismantling of non-White spaces.

**OBJECTIVITY:** The notion of being fact-based and uninfluenced by personal feelings, interpretations, or prejudice.

## THE FOUR C'S OF CHANGEMAKING

**COGENCY:** The state or quality of being clear, logical, and convincing.

**COMPASSION:** Sympathetic concern for the sufferings of others.

**CREATIVITY:** The ability to transcend traditional ideas, rules, patterns, or relationships and creating meaningful new ideas, forms, methods, and/or interpretations.

**COLLABORATION:** The process of two or more people, groups, or entities working in tandem to complete a task, produce a product, or achieve a goal.

# FURTHER READING

# FICTION

*Monster* by Walter Dean Myers
*Lockdown* by Walter Dean Myers
*Dear Martin* by Nic Stone
*Dear Justyce* by Nic Stone
*The Hate U Give* by Angie Thomas
*All American Boys* by Jason Reynolds and Brendan Kiely
*This Is My America* by Kim Johnson
*Anger Is a Gift* by Mark Oshiro
*Tyler Johnson Was Here* by Jay Coles
*Don't Ask Me Where I'm From* by Jennifer De Leon
*We Are Not Free* by Traci Chee
*The Silence That Binds Us* by Joanna Ho
*Barely Missing Everything* by Matt Mendez
*Internment* by Samira Ahmed
*I Am Not Your Perfect Mexican Daughter* by Erika L. Sánchez

# NONFICTION

*Stamped: Racism, Antiracism, and You* by Dr. Ibram X. Kendi and Jason Reynolds
*This Book Is Anti-Racist* by Tiffany Jewell
*We Are Not Yet Equal: Understanding Our Racial Divide* by Dr. Carol Anderson and Tonya Bolden
*It's Trevor Noah: Born a Crime* by Trevor Noah
*Just Mercy (Adapted for Young Adults): A True Story of the Fight for Justice* by Bryan Stevenson
*The 57 Bus: A True Story of Two Teenagers and the Crime That Changed Their Lives* by Dashka Slater
*When They Call You a Terrorist (Young Adult edition): A Story of Black Lives Matter and the Power to Change the World* by Patrisse Khan-Cullors and asha bandele
*The Other Talk: Reckoning with Our White Privilege* by Brendan Kiely

# ABOUT THE AUTHORS

**DR. IBRAM X. KENDI** is the Andrew W. Mellon Professor in the Humanities at Boston University and the founding director of the BU Center for Antiracist Research. Kendi is the author of the National Book Award winner *Stamped from the Beginning: The Definitive History of Racist Ideas in America*; and five #1 *New York Times* bestsellers: *How to Be an Antiracist*; *Stamped: Racism, Antiracism, and You*; co-written with Jason Reynolds; and *Antiracist Baby*, illustrated by Ashley Lukashevsky. His books *How to Raise an Antiracist* and *Goodnight Racism*, illustrated by Cbabi Bayoc, were both instant *New York Times* bestsellers. In 2020, *Time* magazine named Kendi one of the 100 most influential people in the world. He was awarded a 2021 MacArthur Fellowship, popularly known as the Genius Grant.

**NIC STONE** is an Atlanta native and a Spelman College graduate. Her debut novel for young adults, *Dear Martin*, and her debut middle-grade novel, *Clean Getaway*, were both *New York Times* bestsellers. She is also the author of *Odd One Out*, which was an NPR Best Book of the Year and a Rainbow Book List Top Ten selection; *Jackpot, Shuri: A Black Panther Novel*; and *Dear Justyce*. She is one of the authors in the *New York Times* bestselling book *Black Out*, recently optioned as a new anthology television program.

Published in the United States by One World, an
imprint of Random House, a division of Penguin
Random House LLC, New York.

ONE WORLD and colophon are registered trademarks
of Penguin Random House LLC.

Portions of this work were originally published
in *How to Be a (Young) Antiracist* by Ibram X.
Kendi and Nic Stone (New York: Kokila, 2023).

oneworldlit.com

randomhousebooks.com

ISBN 978-0-593-23485-3

Printed in the United States of America

Illustrations by Octavia Ink
Tree icon illustration by Shutterstock.com/g/
rolandtopor
Boxer illustration by Shutterstock.com/g/ZOO.BY

Editors: Sara Neville and Oma Beharry
Designer: Jessie Kaye
Production Editor: Serena Wang
Production Manager: Luisa Francavilla
Compositor: Margaret Discenza and Heather Finn
Copy Editor: Alison Hagge
Marketer: Ayelet Gruenspecht
Publicist: Maria Braeckel

1st Printing

First Edition